Praise for Revela and *Insight Unseen*

"In working with Andrea and her team over the last decade, they have become an integral piece of our organization through the development of our people. They continually challenge our team and force us to be insightful to why we are who we are as individuals and as a company. Andrea pushes us to build our own unique model for success by owning how we got here, identifying who we have become, and challenging us toward where we want to go."

Brian Rasmussen
CEO
Rasmussen Mechanical Services

"She challenges us. Just when you think you've got things figured out, Andrea will ask you another question that helps you consider another perspective. The team at Revela helps us find our blind spots so we can make better decisions. They bring out the best in us."

Terri Gogetap
President
FBG Service Corporation

"She challenges us. It's like putting on someone else's glasses—just when you think you've got things figured out, Andrea will ask another question that helps you see it from another perspective. The team at Revela helps us find our blind spots so we can make better decisions."

Dianne Lozier
Lozier Corporation

"Andrea helped our owners see the difference between owning and managing. Not an easy task when those roles have been one and the same all their life. She helped us see that first line managers are key to culture. She approaches every issue by recognizing that people are human and have reasons for what they do—deep down they all want to contribute. Our challenge in business is to align that with our business goals, or not. Our team is more confident in their management skills from their time with Revela."

Rob Sauer
General Manager
Hill Brothers Transportation

"Andrea always challenges us to think in new ways. Just when we think we have things figured out, she encourages us to consider a different perspective. The team at Revela helps us discover our blind spots so we can make better decisions."

Deb Buhro
CEO
Oxbow Animal Health

"Having lived with blurry leadership vision, I am thankful for the lenses Andrea and her team at Revela have provided our senior leadership team. We "see" more clearly, communicate boldly, and are headed in a strategic direction as a team and organization."

Chris Mehaffey
Scout Executive/CEO
Boy Scouts of America
Mid-America Council

"Andrea's ability to work through complex team dynamics and tie together our individual strengths towards success as one, has strengthened our ability to move forward as a leadership team."

Chris Tointon
President and CEO
YMCA of Greater Omaha

"I've worked with Andrea for nearly twenty years and she has positively impacted our business and our people. She challenges us to avoid the status quo and seek continuous improvement. She encourages us to consider alternative perspectives. She has helped us understand the unique aspects of the varied generations in the workplace and how to maximize productivity and workplace happiness.

Andrea helped guide us through our first iteration of strategic planning, and I've shared her advice to us with many other businesspeople. Her constant encouragement and challenge to me is asking "are you working on your business, or are you working in your business?"

Brad von Gillern
CEO
Lueder Construction

"Andrea gives practical takeaways to specific business problems that make you feel like she's known your business for years. A natural leader and communicator, her wisdom and outlook stand out in pinpointing that "one thing" (blindspot) you may be missing that will take your business to the next level."

Beth Trejo
CEO & Founder
Chatterkick

"TS Banking Group has included Andrea in our senior leadership quarterly meetings for 10+ years. Andrea comes in with questions to make us think deeper on topics and make us think through the "why." She helps us look at things by sometimes being the mirror and other times a window. She is an outsider who has become an insider as to what we do, who we are, and why we are."

Joshua M. Guttau
Chief Executive Officer
TS Banking Group

insight unseen

insight unseen

How To Lead With 20/20 Business Vision

Andrea Fredrickson

THRONE
PUBLISHING GROUP

Copyright © 2019 by Andrea Fredrickson

ISBN: 978-1-949550-24-5
Ebook ISBN: 978-1-949550-25-2

All rights reserved. No part of this book may be reproduced or transmitted in any form or by any means, electronic or mechanical, including photocopying, recording or by any information storage and retrieval system, without permission in writing from the copyright owner. For information on distribution rights, royalties, derivative works or licensing opportunities on behalf of this content or work, please contact the publisher at the address below.

Printed in the United States of America.

Cover Design: Amy Gehling
Copy Editor: Elizabeth Duffy, Certified Legacy Guide

Although the author and publisher have made every effort to ensure that the information and advice in this book was correct and accurate at press time, the author and publisher do not assume and hereby disclaim any liability to any party for any loss, damage, or disruption caused from acting upon the information in this book or by errors or omissions, whether such errors or omissions result from negligence, accident, or any other cause.

Throne Publishing Group
212 S Main Ave, 204B
Sioux Falls, SD 57104
ThronePG.com

To Wayne

Table of Contents

Heads Up! . . . . *xiii*

Start Here . . . . *xv*

PART ONE: Revela

1   Lenses That Matter 3

2   Applying Your Lenses To Any Situation 17

PART TWO: Lenses in Action

3   The Visionary 29

4   The Strategist 39

5   The Architect 47

6   The Taskmaster 57

7   The Truthsayer 67

8   The Team Builder 75

9	The Coach. 85
10	The Technician (AKA: Your Default Lens) 93
11	The Ultimate Action Plan. 99

About the Author *103*

About the Company *105*

Heads Up!

Some books are written for reading only. Others, like this one, are written to be worked. *Insight Unseen* is a tool meant to help you identify blind spots in your own leadership practices and pinpoint what's missing on your team. You can read this with the intention of applying it, but if you don't, it's just more information stuck in your head.

If you are truly serious about making the most of this leadership trek, we have some resources that will enhance your ability to apply the ideas referenced in this book. Check out www.InsightUnseen.com for tools, articles, and tips to help you start taking action.

Start Here

Imagine a student straining to see his teacher's notes each day in class. He listens, engages, and puts in the work, but for the life of him, all of the words are a blur. No matter how hard he squints, the letters and numbers stay fuzzy squiggles, and he just can't seem to see what others are able to.

If any of us met this student, we'd all offer the same suggestion: "Why don't you try some glasses?"

When the right lenses are in place, everything comes into sharp focus, and the struggle of vision vanishes. The teacher's notes are easily read and the student's performance can skyrocket—all simply because he can finally see clearly.

In business, we get stuck in a similar phenomenon. We each have blind spots, areas naturally blurry to us. And strain as we might, until we have the right lenses ourselves, we're achieving less than our full potential.

I wrote this book to offer those lenses to business leaders with a similar nagging feeling that somehow, somewhere, they're missing something. That there's a less-siloed view of the organization as a whole, but they need to look beyond their own horizon of responsibility to grasp it. But here's the problem: they're insanely busy fighting fires and doing damage control. Their schedule is reactive. They're sick of politicking and working days that constantly bleed far beyond eight hours.

Does any of this sound familiar?

If this sounds anything like you or leaders in your organization, I wrote this book for you. The goal is simple: to give you the tools to see your business with 20/20 vision. It will act as a sort of optometrist for your leadership. In the pages ahead, there are viewpoints you've never considered blended with some you already know. After all, you've gotten to where you are because of your natural strengths, work ethic, and genuine skill. However, I don't want you to get stuck in the trap that you already know all of this. I'm going to ask you to put your natural lens, your expertise, on hold while you consider each of the lenses and how I've defined them.

What if You Just Need Glasses?

Just like the optometrist asks, "One, or two?" narrowing in on 20/20 vision, the strategies and ideas are meant to dial in your business vision. I'm going to suggest a radically new way of growing your leadership, influence, and output: instead of squinting, just get some glasses!

You will be introduced to a profoundly effective set of leadership tools. The Eight Lenses have been developed over decades of working with thousands of people in every business context imaginable.

A quick word of warning, though. Reading is superficial until you reflect and take action. This book is meant to be worked—not simply to be read. You lose all the value if you never put these things into practice. And what is the value?

Achieving your full potential as a leader and organization through the power of 20/20 business vision.

If you're ready to receive an entirely new way to see your team's strengths and gain insight into your blind spots, turn the page. Greater impact and results always follow clarity. And clarity is found through The Eight Lenses.

PART ONE

Revela

Lenses That Matter

My first great entrepreneurial lesson wasn't taught in college or soaked up as I navigated the business world. It actually happened during my childhood, on the streets of a small southwestern Iowa town as I ran errands with my father. A new business owner himself, my father had the insight and wisdom to know his role was about more than business—it was about community.

With the watchful eyes of a child, I witnessed him tie the success of his business with the success of our small town. They were not mutually exclusive in his eyes. If the business were to be successful, the town had to be successful as well. That means he understood the need to invest in the people around him with the same intensity he invested in his new business. And if you know any passionate business owner, you know just how much he poured into both.

For those of you unfamiliar with small towns, it's pretty easy to get to know people, but my dad went out of his way to develop relationships. He purposefully sought out ways to help other businesses be successful, and he did it with humility. He encouraged, gave advice, and supported other local businesses, and then he backed it up with his actions. From the hardware store to the grocery store, to the laundromat and the hair salon that opened on Main Street, we shopped and serviced our lives with local businesses.

In return, people respected him, and they listened as he guided and offered advice. As a young girl, I can still hear my father asking people about different aspects of their business, how they were going about their business, and most importantly, why? What was at the heart of their business, and how did they operate? How quickly did they restock inventory? How did they market? What did the future look like? It made them think, re-evaluate, and refine what was already working. He learned. They learned. It was one business owner helping another and it was a lesson I'll never forget.

A Humble Growth Process

I didn't fully grasp the importance of his lessons while we walked the sidewalks of our hometown streets. But years later, his lessons became the foundation of my own work to help businesses strengthen, refine, and inspire within the walls of their organization.

In the late 1980s when we first launched our company, now known as Revela, I continued to draw wisdom from my father. Again, it was not uncommon for us to spend Saturday mornings together. We would start on separate projects, but oftentimes ended up back in a brainstorming session—me in the chair in his office bombarding him with questions and ideas.

Here, my ideas began to crystalize. Local, smaller, and mid-sized businesses in the Midwest faced the same challenges all businesses across the country face, and they needed the perspective and insight my father had taught me so long ago.

As we worked with more and more businesses, we started to identify patterns within organizations that produced results (both good and bad). We could identify strengths—individuals with solid skills, experience, talent, and enthusiasm. But we also identified gaps that were holding companies back. Sometimes there was no one setting the vision or direction. For others, there was no accountability for goals. We saw executives leading groups of people, but not true teams.

Revela, and the trajectory of my career, took off right there. Revela could be that much needed outside perspective for businesses and organizations. We use the same process today that we started more than three decades ago—to walk alongside businesses and help them solve problems, grow, develop their community, and excel in their niche. It all goes back to those first lenses my father helped me look through as a child.

As I'll show throughout the rest of this book, lenses are powerful business tools that help us see reality. Just like getting glasses from the optometrist, that blurry chart becomes crystal clear when we look through the right lenses. The word *Revela* in Spanish means to reveal or discover, and that's exactly what the lenses help us do. And one of the first things the right lenses help us see are red flags that may have been flying under the radar—sometimes for years.

How To See Hidden Red Flags

When we work with companies, we don't simply identify the problem and throw out a solution. We create an atmosphere to provide opportunities for leaders and staff to discover ideas and solutions themselves. We help to shift their mindset, enabling leaders to embrace reality and make better decisions for clients and customers.

When we started working with businesses, we discovered something very quickly. Frequently, the problems companies think they have are actually present because they're lacking something else or sometimes, someone else.

There are many red flags that can indicate something is missing in your business. Here are the three most common:

1. **Reactionary patterns.**

    If your business is only reactionary to problems or challenges, you will trip over every minor bump in the road. If there is no foresight, you cannot anticipate new hurdles, provide innovative services, or set goals. Clients ask for services and you simply react. If you are not taking charge, it's a sign that you lack a Visionary—someone who sees opportunities, or a Taskmaster—someone who holds everyone accountable.

2. **Dysfunctional teams.**

    The second red flag that you are missing something is a dysfunctional team. Maybe you have people who have been with you forever, but in truth, they are functioning more as a swim team and not as a baseball team. They're not working together. They are working for themselves. These types of teams, whether we recognize it or not, can be detrimental to your ability to move the business forward.

3. **No succession plan.**

    When there is no succession plan, the senior leadership team is not developing their bench. If it's a private or family business, what happens to the business if something happens to the owner or senior executive? It's a difficult situation if the patriarch or matriarch is the person with all the contacts and relationships and is also the Visionary. Who will be ready to carry the torch when the current leader is no longer there or able?

These are simply three of the many, many red flags we commonly uncover. And this happens all the time. A company engages us to help solve a specific problem or help them with a project like strategic planning or leadership development. They have already self-diagnosed the problem. But when we spend time with them, we usually discover there are missing lenses.

Revealing Blind Spots

I still think of one new business that was run by a young woman. It was a leap of faith to start the business, and she was running it by sheer gut instinct. She was looking through only a couple of lenses. She could see the possibilities from a Visionary perspective. She could see what everything could be, but not what it should be. This meant everything was an option and there were no set processes or systems to follow.

When we partnered with her, she didn't understand her margins, that her team desperately needed coaching and professional development, and that sometimes healthy confrontation is a necessary part of leadership.

Because of her blind spots, she was leading a group of people, not a team. This business owner was a master of the product—both in development, research, and market—but she was running off course.

And she's not alone! There are millions of business owners each year who start with the right heart, the right motive, and the right ideas. But their best laid plans are in danger of failing or flopping if they can't see the entire picture.

The best part of our job is witnessing business leaders discover where they have blind spots and then moving to reveal them. It's supporting the journey where the missing lenses are discovered within an organization, where the perfect puzzle pieces are locked in so you can become better at what you do.

Successfully Stuck

Surprisingly, success can be a double-edged sword. I can't tell you how many times executives or business leaders are *successfully* stuck, meaning they have historically been successful and are now unwilling to cast a vision for the future that would be outside the parameters of what they have been doing for so long. There are four areas this most commonly happens, and they all stem from blind spots.

Comfort

It's a place of comfort, a fear of the unknown. A company may be refining processes and creating more efficiencies, but they're growing neither their top-line revenue nor their market share. They aren't expanding their product offerings. This eventually leads to their customers leaving and the people in the company blaming them for their lack of success.

How does a company get to this place? They found success early on, got into a groove, and now are so far in the weeds they've lost perspective. They believe historical success is a predictor of future success. That's a dangerous place to be.

At Revela, we passionately believe that untapped leadership skills can be discovered and developed no matter the age or maturity of the company or organization. Reflection is always healthy, and sometimes all you need is a little nudge to step outside your comfort zone.

Lack of Focus

On the other end, a company can be unfocused. When this happens, they change directions often because the Visionary is chasing squirrels. Their team waits to be told what to do because they know they're expected to follow the whims of leadership anyway! The lack of consistency erodes the foundation of the business.

The constant shifting also means there is no clear discipline. If the only commitment is to try new things, you can never become great at any one thing. Improvement is always needed, but constantly shifting focus is unhealthy. As Jim Collins writes in his book *Built To Last*, it's possible to preserve the core and stimulate progress. He doesn't say to constantly shift the focus, though, because that's the perfect recipe for mediocrity.

High Turnover

A lack of perspective also invites the damaging effects of high turnover. A major reason high turnover happens is because expectations are unclear and results are not rewarded. High performers grow frustrated because of a system that is sluggish or confusing. When expectations are unclear, or the direction of the expectations change too often, they grow unhappy.

When something negative happens, leaders often find reasons to justify or excuse the misstep. They're not looking through the Truthsayer lens (more on this ahead). It's a problem that has persisted through the decades. Justifications, rationalizations, excuses, and anything but the truth is simply a lack of integrity.

Fractionated Teams

Another weak area we see is fractionated teams. If there is no trust, people will look out for themselves. The ego is a powerful thing when it is the focus of decision-making for each individual. The ego will operate on survival mode—me against the rest of the world. It says you must protect yourself at all costs, always be right, and never show weakness. If you have a team of people who are led by this type of ego, you'll never have a cohesive team. You will also never have a team looking for the customer win instead of the personal victory.

Here's an analogy I use often: Swim teams score individually to contribute to the team, but baseball teams work together. A batter bunts, rather than always swinging for the fences. Or, if you prefer another sports analogy, basketball players often assist while not always scoring the points.

The Eight Lenses

Team sports remind me of my dad and his desire—even as a new business owner who needed to make his mark—to set himself apart from the competition and hit the ground running. He took the high road and saw his business as part of the greater good to the community. He was never concerned about receiving credit for his work, but understood the greater principle that if those around him prospered, he would too.

It's that same purposefulness I learned from my father I now encourage you to use as you work to better understand each of these lenses. We're careful to analyze and embrace each one of these because the more comfortable you become with each perspective, the stronger your contributions and decision-making abilities will become within your business. Let's take a brief look at each one.

The Visionary Lens

If you're looking through the Visionary Lens, your eye is trained on the horizon and challenging the status quo. Your ideas are future-oriented. The weakness of this lens is the resistance to declare plans. You prefer fuzzier language where there is room for interpretation. "What I see is ... Let's think about ... Have we considered? ..." And yet, we rely on this lens greatly to help us get out of ruts, challenge the status quo, and grow the business because its true strength is forcing us to lift our heads up and look to the future.

The Strategist Lens

This lens determines the boundaries of where we will and won't go. This lens encourages critical thinking and helps manage the tension between growth and resources. The Strategist Lens reminds us to balance needs and availability so we don't over-commit and exhaust our resources, including time, funding, and staff. This lens makes the tough decisions, meaning we can and have to say no to things. The downside is that drawing hard lines can create tension with other lenses—like the Visionary. And at times, this lens can err on the side of viewing operations too narrowly. Tunnel vision is always the danger here. The balance with the Strategist Lens is that they provide much-needed clarity when there are so many options and dreams afloat.

The Architect Lens

The Architect Lens builds the foundation, the structure, and the support beams for the business or organization. This lens provides the systems and processes required to achieve results and meet goals. This lens is naturally organized in its thinking, but the blind spot is putting a plan into place without considering negative downstream effects. This lens is needed because their consistent design ensures we have consistent results. Standardization can be a very good thing when done well.

The Taskmaster Lens

This lens is all about the deadline and delivering on promises. The Taskmaster sets the expectations, knows the expectations, and lives the expectations, providing a backbone for accountability. The Taskmaster believes each person should rise to the challenge, and no one should be left behind.

The downside could be a harmful lack of flexibility. This lens places deadlines and accountability ahead of all else, sometimes at the expense of people, long-term vision, or unexpected hurdles.

This lens is an important leg of the operation, as it holds the line. Things get done when life is viewed through the Taskmaster Lens.

The Truthsayer Lens

There is nothing more illuminating to the current reality than the Truthsayer Lens. This lens consistently dismisses evidence that doesn't support the truth and is able to discern fact from fiction or opinion. This lens puts a spotlight on the right and sorts out the wrong. This lens is about doing the research and analyzing the data—always in a search for truth. A potential blind spot for this lens is using truth as a hammer. A Truthsayer Lens means encompassing the wisdom to spot the truth and using it to better the situation and others.

It's important and needed because it keeps people dealing in reality, not in fantasy. You can't know forward is really forward without this lens.

The Team Builder Lens

This lens creates a cohesive team that can work interdependently to meet goals. The Team Builder Lens provides a view from the ground and the top-level, meaning this lens reduces drama and office politics. This lens can squash unhealthy conflict and help team members relate to each other more effectively.

The downside of a Team Builder Lens is the danger it will become too people-focused, as opposed to results-focused. It's easy to get off track from the goals and vision if too much attention is spent on managing people's drama.

A team without a Team Builder Lens is missing an important component, however. It's needed to help people communicate, collaborate, empathize, and celebrate. A business that supports its people is stronger from within, and therefore stronger in its mission.

The Coach Lens

The Coach Lens is the perfect lens for one-on-one people training. This lens develops and encourages people individually. The Coach Lens has a great perspective of seeing the strengths and weaknesses in each team member and drawing out the best in each person so the collective team is always at its peak.

A downside for this lens is it can overstep boundaries—point out too much truth and not allow people to fail so they can learn from their own mistakes.

Still, the good far outweighs the bad with this lens. The Coach Lens provides continuous development, training, and encouragement. It ensures each individual is producing at maximum capacity, and that they are always learning.

The Technician Lens

This lens is viewing the issue at hand through the eyes of an expert. The strength of the Technician Lens is the mastery of a subject or task, which allows this lens to view the challenges facing the company with specific knowledge and experience.

The downside is being so far into the zone of your subject matter expertise that this lens doesn't consider the importance of subject matter experts in areas outside of your knowledge.

This lens is crucial to a smooth operation. The Technician Lens sets your company apart from everything else because no one does what you do or knows what you know as well as you do in the business.

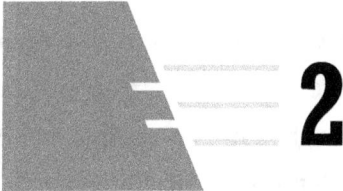

Applying Your Lenses To Any Situation

President John F. Kennedy was convinced we were going to the moon, and in an historic speech before a joint session of Congress in 1961, he had us on the edge of our seats with a bold promise.

"We choose to go to the moon," he pronounced, and it was his decisive language that set the United States on a course to outer space, buoyed by Kennedy's belief we would do it before the decade ended. Two years later, Kennedy was assassinated, and eight years after the speech, NASA's Apollo 11 mission landed the first humans on the moon.

Kennedy's remarks were more than a visionary statement. It was a deep conviction coupled with the authority to say it was going to happen. It was a Strategist Lens, and much like Kennedy spoke about the moon with urgency and destiny, a Strategist should evoke the same in their team.

But just like Kennedy's powerful statement to propel us into outer space, it takes more than ballsy statements to move an operation forward. All eight lenses were required to take us to the moon. Just imagine the incredible undertaking, from all backgrounds and perspectives, to get us there.

The Strategist Lens, while indelibly important to the course of a company, is just one of the lenses needed to operate a healthy, long-term operation. Every lens is equally valuable, viable, and needed.

Keep in mind, lenses are the perspective through which we see the situation and the people in front of us. When we view our team through each lens, there's no need to pigeonhole people into only one category. People can switch lenses during any conversation or in different seasons of their life's work. Focus on the lens and how that transforms thinking and the decisions you need to make rather than the personal characteristics of the people you view.

When you neglect to look through all eight lenses, you're operating your business on a one-dimensional level. When you consider the perspective of every lens in your decision-making processes, you're giving yourself a robust view of every situation. You're giving yourself 20/20 vision.

Using the Lenses

These eight lenses should be used by every executive team, and considered tools in every situation. But just as you don't need a jackhammer to cook an omelet or a spatula to fix a tire, every lens may not be necessary in every situation.

When we're looking at executing the plan of the future, a person needs to be able to shift through each of the lenses throughout that cycle. Consider each lens and then view your work through whatever is appropriate in each situation.

By first considering each lens, you are reducing your blind spots, and as a result, you will be a better-rounded, dynamic leader who can build trust with the team you're on or the team you lead. Your organization will have fewer disappointing moments as the result of looking through each lens before making a decision or setting a process in motion.

You will have the ability to solve problems on a deeper level by looking through all the lenses. And you will have a much broader perspective of where your organization is going because you're approaching each decision or challenge from all angles.

I like to think of it as having the pilot's view. The people on the ground see only one runway. But the pilot has the great advantage of additional information from the control tower, a cockpit of tools to help him land, and a bird's-eye view from the air.

When you take the time to process decisions utilizing all the lenses, you have improved situational awareness. Simply put, you have the best view.

This is especially advantageous when there's something that's growing or changing (or should be). When you consider every lens, you are keenly aware of which lens provides the clearest view of how to move forward. There may be a situation when there is more focus on one lens.

For instance, the business is kicking off a new product line, and the Architect Lens may be the sole focus. Alongside that, we also need to be Visionary or creative in what the plan looks like for the future of the product, but the Architect Lens provides the clearest and most efficient path to our goal.

When we're launching a new product line, we need to be Strategic because we don't have access to every resource out there. And while we recognize that the Architect Lens is our focus, a handful of our team members need to be given feedback in order to fully execute on this new product line, incorporating the Coach Lens.

An Orchestra of Tools

It's an orchestra of sorts. Different instruments will be called upon during particular songs throughout the duration of a musical performance.

The next time you are in a meeting, embrace the fact you have these lenses to look through, and take advantage of it. Take a minute to orient yourself based on the agenda. What is the objective of this particular conversation and how can I adjust my viewpoint to accomplish what we set out to do?

For example, do we need to limit our scope? Do we need to set boundaries? Do we need to move more quickly?

It helps you not simply default to your strength lens. Instead, look through each lens at the beginning of the conversation, then reflect back. Be honest. Did you default to your strengths lens? Do you need to go back and reconsider the conversation through the other lenses?

This approach is your best toolbox. The lenses are dynamic, and the more you can see through them, the greater value they provide. They provide balance so things aren't forgotten or overlooked, which is vital on every executive team. The eight lenses form a solid, holistic framework. They blur the lines among subject matter experts because they gently force the consideration of others.

I have been asked about the lenses in relation to various popular personality assessments, which are tools often used in the workplace and organizations. The two systems are supplemental. Remember, however, that people of all personalities can use the perspective of the lenses at different seasons and in different situations. Utilizing the lenses is not about fitting the right personality into the right job, but approaching each decision and situation holistically.

Versatility is one of the greatest strengths of the lens perspective. You need to be able to activate all lenses at different times. You never know when a situation will change, and you can't predict every conversation. You need to be able to think on your feet and with a familiarity of the lenses so you can change perspective quickly when it's needed.

This is what will make you a stronger leader. Your team needs you to be able to make a quick assessment and adjust accordingly.

Throw Out Old Beliefs

Want to ride a backwards bike? You better clear your calendar. A popular YouTuber re-engineered one of America's greatest classic pastimes—riding a bike—and turned it into a lesson on neuroplasticity (the ability of our brains to modify themselves). By simply reversing the handlebars on his bike—making right turns left and left turns right—he demonstrated the cognitive ability to learn and relearn through a challenging and lengthy process to teach himself again.

Learning to ride a backwards bike took the YouTuber eight months to master, and the ensuing videos posted by people who took on his challenge to do the same are quite entertaining.

On a more serious note, it's a subtle reminder to us. Our brains are wired to depend on habits. Scientists break it down this way: thoughts repeated create neural pathways. But when you first started riding a bike, you didn't have a preset neural pathway. You learned the bike-riding skills, and all your skills, through the development of myelin, which is an insulating layer of tissue that wraps itself around nerves.

When you practice a skill, your nerves receive signals to grow myelin. The more myelin, the more muscle memory you develop. The process is repeated over and over until you have mastered whatever you set out to do.

That brings us to your brain. As a leader, you have formed beliefs through your habits of thought. When you do or think something over and over again it becomes automatic, unless you bring it to your consciousness.

People depend on their habits of thought to get through their day. I don't have to think about breathing or tying my shoes. The engineer on YouTube who reworked his bike took months to rewire his brain to ride his backwards bike, but his young son accomplished it in just a couple weeks. Why is that? Because the man had already formed his traditional bike-riding habits. The boy had not.

Habits of thought, like riding a bike the proper way, take you back to your natural strengths (or lenses). But to grow, you must challenge or disrupt the very habits you have maintained for so long.

To question or challenge a habit stretches the mind and disrupts how you think. Disruption is where you grow. I'm not talking about chaos, but disruption. When you have made decisions at your company for years with the same thought patterns and considerations, it will take a new way of thinking to pause and look through each lens before proceeding.

Do it enough times, and it will become your new thought pattern. Like riding that backwards bike, it won't come naturally at first. New thought patterns require repetition, a desire to make a change for the better even as your brain neurons are firing up to do what you've always done. It takes time. Like I said, clear your calendar.

And in the end, you may choose to return to the way it was, but you can't unlearn or unknow something, so you are stretched regardless of whether the change is permanent. In the case of the lenses, I challenge you to step out of the status quo and embrace the new perspective. Growth can be uncomfortable, but it's necessary.

To better understand, simply reflect on the trajectory of your life. How are you a different person from who you were a decade ago? You might still have some of the same habits of thought or action, but more than likely, there are numerous things that have changed. You have grown.

"I Wish I'd Known…"

How many times do we hear someone say, "I wish I had known then what I know now?" Ever said that yourself? Looking through the perspective of these eight lenses is a path to stop saying that so often.

If you are of the belief that you have already grown, already been stretched, don't need to make any changes, you're not in a growth mindset. You're not truly considering stretching your leadership vision. These are old beliefs you should abandon.

Your current habits aren't wrong—they're likely incomplete. Don't throw away everything you've learned. Instead, build on your strengths and then embrace this strategic disruption so you can grow.

If you're a leader worth your salt, you are in a constant state of improvement and development. You have not become the leader you were meant to be—yet. That little one-syllable word defines the possibility of the future. You are not there—yet. You're on your way. You're going to take action.

You have not reached the moon—yet. But you're about to.

Time to Go to Work

Simply reading the chapters is not using the information. You've got to put the information to work. At the end of each chapter we've provided a few questions, each designed to get you thinking. You'll be tempted to just read the questions without taking any action, but don't. We want you to stop, reflect and write down the answers before you go to the next chapter. After all, taking in information is not how you become better. It's reflecting, challenging, and practicing new skills that helps you improve.

1. After an initial introduction to each lens, which lens do you suspect you need to give the most attention to?
2. On a scale of 1–5, one meaning no interest and five meaning totally committed, to what level are you determined to disrupt how you look at situations to benefit your team?

PART TWO

Lenses in Action

3

The Visionary

If you've ever been to the Great Wall of China, you might have noticed this impressive archaeological feat is punctuated by watchtowers. The towers, ten to twelve meters high, performed a crucial role during the Ming Dynasty and many others. Soldiers could see the enemy long before those on the ground had a clue someone was approaching.

The view from the top is simply the best vantage point. Someone who has the ability to look out over the lay of the land with discernment—whether physically standing on the Wall of China or working as a valued member of your team—is crucial in key moments.

The Visionary Lens is marked by an ability to keep one's head high so as not to be bogged down by details of a project. Someone looking through this lens will have a desire to look ahead—way ahead. They consider the possibilities, ask the questions of "have you considered?" or "what about?" or "wouldn't it be great if?"

The Visionary Lens is discerning, innovative, and creative. They dream, and those dreams expand and challenge what people imagine is possible beyond the status quo.

This lens gathers bits of information and finds the constellations from seemingly random clumps of stars. They are always on the path to learn more and to synthesize information in new ways. It's the choreographers at Cirque du Soleil—creating acrobatic and balletic beauty from scratch. This lens puts existing things in fresh combinations to create something profound.

A Visionary is always dreaming—BIG. Ideas on a grand scale, all the time, can be a downfall. It can overwhelm you, restraining you from settling on one direction and moving toward it.

The person looking through this lens must remember, it's okay to constantly challenge the status quo, but not to dilute focus.

Imagine a ship constantly changing destinations. All you do is travel in a circle, never getting anywhere at best. At worst, you change courses too quickly and tip over.

The Hallmark of the Visionary Lens

The hallmark of a great Visionary is asking bold questions. They think of the big picture and progression—what are we doing in a year, in five years, in ten? They are not intimidated or hindered by the idea of legacy and where your business or organization will be many years down the road. They are curious and optimistic, and consistently ask "What if? ..."

Looking through the Visionary Lens is really about feeling safe and comfortable enough to dream. I think of Alan Mullaly, who reimagined the Ford Motor Company. Mullaly is credited with saving America's flagship motor company as it was careening toward financial ruin in 2008. Bill Ford recognized the vision and believed in Mullaly enough to let him dream. It paid off big time for the company.

The Visionary Lens is also about learning. Nothing is irrelevant. The Visionary has a sponge-like ability to absorb information and synthesize it in a way that moves the company forward. They are, after all, laser-focused on moving to the future.

Someone peering through this lens will discover a voracious appetite for information. They could be someone who gets ready in the morning while listening to podcasts and audiobooks. On the way to work, it's another audiobook or a news station. They listen with purpose, and they absorb information with abandon—whether it be at a conference or a mention of something interesting from a friend at the coffee shop. They enjoy accumulating information and knowledge, not knowing when the information will be used. The Visionary synthesizes all the information and puts it together in fresh ways.

Someone operating inside the Visionary Lens exhibits an incredible amount of discipline. Ironically, they can struggle with restraint, not always knowing the best time to bring ideas forward.

They are not likely to get derailed if no one jumps onboard with their idea or doesn't agree. They are confident in their abilities and recognize not all of their ideas will be used.

Frustrations and Insights

The frustrations of a Visionary can be stirred by a lack of enthusiasm from other team members who might feel their ideas are too far-fetched or not possible. There's nothing they hate more than hearing, "Yeah, but ..." or the sighs of fellow team members who don't have the patience to hear another idea or pitch.

They want—need—their ideas to be listened to, at least, to be considered and taken seriously.

Someone looking through this lens despises the detail work. Working out the specifics is better left to someone else. To the Visionary, details are drudgery.

What they love is seeing opportunity and the potential in a project. They often wonder, *Am I supposed to do something with this bit of information, or just take it in?* They love making connections and creating grand schemes. They may do nothing with what they have created, but it's the process of thinking and building ideas that fulfills them.

The key results they are driving include positive change, challenging the status quo, and creating energy for the team.

The Lookouts

If some of China's historic dynasties did not have the watch towers that now stand out from the Great Wall, we would be reading a different history of that country. It's the same with the Visionary Lens on your team. They do more than look out for the enemy—their insight is incredibly valuable because they look at the places where no one else is focused.

Many of the other lenses have their noses to the ground doing their own valuable work. But the Visionary has their eyes on the sky. They don't wait for the market to demand new services. They already have ideas for what the customer will want, sometimes before the customer even knows they want it.

That's important because markets continually shift, and shifting markets are not going away. More so, appetites and demands are always changing. A Visionary Lens means working proactively and not simply reacting to needs. A Visionary is a master at recognizing the relevant gaps before anyone else. They want to know where the tension, rub, or gap is that needs to be filled.

JFK's desire was to develop a legitimate space program before Russia. He wanted the U.S. to be known as an interstellar power before them. A Visionary like JFK will add energy and vigor, and their discernment allows them to look beyond their own subject matter expertise and consider the entire company's needs from all perspectives. They understand how ideas have cause-and-effect across disciplines.

A Visionary is needed at specific key points during the life of your company. They are needed when times are good, before they start to slide. At this point, they will ask, "What is the next thing customers need and will value?" They are needed whenever you're creating a business or department strategy, when they will challenge the thinking of what you'll do different or differently than your industry or competitor. Before the decisions are made, it's crucial to have this lens remind you of the possibilities.

Before you set strategy, this lens has already considered the wider possibilities. If you want to create energy in an organization—or get out of a rut—then you need Visionary thinking. This lens becomes so valuable *before* you get stuck.

It's Never Too Late

If you're already stuck, and there's no energy, it's not too late to benefit from a view from the watchtower. Be open to admitting that you didn't have or consider this lens, and recognize you need it now.

When you personally lack the perspective of the Visionary Lens, you are not maximizing growth for the area for which you're responsible. You are more than likely reactive, rather than proactive, and you have limited ability to advance in whatever role you are in currently. Chances are, you're going to hit a ceiling.

If no one is looking through the Visionary Lens within your company, the entire organization is reactionary. Your reputation will suffer because you are not viewed as forward-thinking, innovative, or rising to the top as leaders. You might be acquired by someone who is growing faster than you.

One of the greatest dangers is that you create a culture void of vision. When this lens isn't used, those who love to try new things will move on, which creates poor retention and high turnover. The organization perpetuates an atmosphere where people tend to get stuck in old habits and when change is necessary, it's harder to get the whole organization to shift.

Break With Routine

If you have recognized that you are lacking the Visionary Lens, the first action step is to get out of your routines. One of the most efficient ways to do this is creating a purposeful thought pattern that includes looking at things from different perspectives. In fact, it's much like the parable of the blind men describing their first experience with an elephant.

As the story goes, a group of blind men come across an elephant for the first time and conceptualize what the elephant is like by touching it. Each blind man feels a different part of the elephant's body, but only one part, such as the side, the tail, or the tusk. They then describe the elephant, but their descriptions are wildly different based on their limited experience.

As you're reading or listening to any media, consider both how it applies to you and your world *and* how it could be used in other ways or for other people. Think about how the information applies to a future state or future possibility. How does it connect with what you were just listening to or reading? Switch it up. Read and/or listen to things that are outside of your normal space. Go to events or conferences that address ideas and concepts not within your expertise. Find new people to talk to and engage with. All these exercises will expand your thinking.

It's Time to Dream

Let yourself dream. Ask yourself the question, "If I wanted to [fill in the blank], what are the craziest ways to make this happen?" A silly exercise we use is by giving people a paperclip and asking what are all of the ways we could use a paperclip. One team we worked with came up with 50!

When you're working to create the future of a company, the Visionary Lens is critical. Without this lens, teams tend to identify small iterations or shifts in what they are already doing. Instead, the Visionary Lens challenges you to consider the questions. What problems or friction points do we want to solve or remove for our customer? They are not restricted by history, equipment, resources, or people. Dream. The other lenses will address the challenges.

Ask yourself a prospective question, like, "What if we want to take down a competitor? How would we do it? And when we do take down our competitor, then what?" Another approach is to ask yourself, "What would make something we already do better?" Nothing is too wild. The Visionary Lens doesn't limit while dreaming.

Identify someone on your team or in your life who looks through this lens naturally and ask them how they think. Watch them in action. Take them to lunch. Be open to learn.

Words are so powerful. When someone in your team is in this lens, say, "Yes, and ..." instead of "Yeah, but..." The first allows the team to help the Visionary rather than crushing why something won't work. Can ideas be developed rather than contracted? "Yes and..." is a way to keep ideas from being shut down while inviting refinement.

There's a good chance they're on to something, and you'll benefit from listening and walking through the idea with them.

Develop Your Visionary Lens

Stop and reflect on the following questions. We encourage you to take time to build a plan to develop your Visionary lens before reading the next chapter.

1. In every meeting for the next two weeks, search for who's looking through the Visionary lens. Write down their names.
2. Next, observe and journal, what is it that they're doing? What questions are they asking?
3. Finally, plan for two things that will take you out of your routine for the next thirty days. How will you implement them?

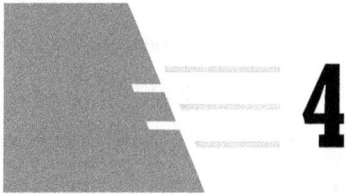

4

The Strategist

Martin Luther King Jr. had a dream, but that dream wouldn't have gone anywhere without the strategy and insight of civil rights leaders around the country who took up arms against racism.

A Strategist will help establish the blueprint for success. This lens helps define the sandbox we're going to play in by putting a clear mark around what is possible. This lens defines priorities.

This lens is powerful—it's a place where we can excel and make the biggest difference. A Strategist sees all the balloons in the sky—the hopes and dreams and "what ifs"—and plucks the right ones from the abyss and holds them firmly so they are not floating away anymore. It's the first step toward action.

The Strategist recognizes multiple great ideas, but reminds us that we can't be all things to all people. They pinpoint exactly where we're going to make the biggest difference and their greatest work is identifying the resources.

The Strategist Lens forces us to decide where and how we're going to make an impact. It provides focus and clarity on using resources well to achieve our desired results. It means we don't waste our resources. It's a commitment to making the tough decisions about who you want to make happy because once you set perimeters, not everyone will be inside the walls. If you're in the sandbox—in other words, if you're the target audience—this will work well for you. If not, this isn't for you and that's OK.

Strengths of the Strategist

The Strategist defines who we are and who we aren't. In my experience, one without the other spells disaster. You have to know who you are and who you aren't in order to move forward. Saying no to somebody, or something, is as important as who or what you say yes to.

There's clarity when looking through the Strategist Lens. The sky is not full of wild idea balloons anymore. The Strategist has plucked down the best, and they are firmly in your hand.

One of the key skills of the Strategist Lens is their ability to think critically, examining information to make a decision. They are constantly asking questions that need to be answered. Oftentimes, they ask tough questions that refine in order to establish a clear strategy.

The Strategist Lens does have blind spots, particularly when it comes to setting a strategy and being married to it. A strategy may have to be revisited and assessed, but a Strategist may see things too narrowly and resist that.

A Strategist Lens can create tunnel vision. A strategy that is too narrowly defined is limiting and doesn't allow for growth or the natural shifting of the market, customers, economy, or staffing. On the other hand, a strategy that is too broad will be confusing, use too many resources, and lack the clarity and focus that leads to success.

The struggle is managing the tension between moving forward, our biggest impact, and our resources. A Strategist Lens allows a buffer between the Visionary and everyone else. They are the funnel that absorbs the ideas and weeds out what will not work, and what will most likely move the needle forward.

How to Spot the Strategist Lens

The Strategist Lens is easy to spot. The person looking through this lens is often asking pointed questions to identify the greatest impact. This lens is all about figuring out who we're going to have the greatest impact on. Who is at the center of our bell curve? Who is not at the center? If the ideas at the table are too inclusive of everyone, this lens forces the focus and eliminates people who simply don't fit the target.

As an example, years ago when my father and I were first starting our business, he and I knew there was a need for coaching, strategic planning, and developing leaders in a lot of companies. (A lot!) But we also knew that we couldn't be all things to all people and at the time, there were only two of us. We had to decide who our target audience would be so we could manage and focus our time to make the most impact. We chose privately-owned or family businesses with multiple locations who are growing or in the midst of change and believe in their people. It took us several conversations to get to that decision, but it has served us well.

Once the Strategist Lens finds that answer, they laser-focus on the strategy that will serve the audience. The Strategic Lens consistently reminds us of where we want to spend our resources, and is quick to remind us of our priorities and that we can't do everything or be all things to all people.

Their thought process is rooted in creating the simplest message with the most clarity of what the parameters are to get to where we want to go. The Strategist doesn't need to solve *how* we're going to get there—that's down the road.

Someone looking through a Strategist Lens will behave with intensity at times. They are very good listeners and in turn, do a lot of critical thinking. They ask hard questions, and they force a team to make a concrete decision.

What Makes Strategists Thrive (and Hide)

The Strategist Lens thrives on creating a decisive plan. We will create a culture that promotes upward mobility to those who have a growth mindset, or we will grow our business by focusing on family-owned and private businesses within one hundred miles that are embarking on change. A Strategist Lens is about conviction and being clear with those around you. You gain a healthy sense of the direction of the organization or company when you're around someone working through this lens.

What a Strategist hates most is mud. They don't like fuzzy, unclear ideas, and they get agitated when people complicate or muddy the waters over a decision that was already made. They don't like the boundaries to be expanded or moved after they have been set—particularly if there is no solid evidence to support a change or move.

The Strategist Lens is about taking the time to research, think, analyze, and support a decision with viable data. Team members who push a plan or change course without data to back it up will not be on the same page as a Strategist.

Hope or a gut feeling as a strategy is the worst kind of way to move forward, according to this lens. They see in black and white and prefer to let a plan (one backed with viable data) play out a little to prove if it is making progress or not. A Strategist Lens avoids making decisions completely on feelings.

The Strategist Lens loves clarity—a simple, straightforward, clear way toward an outcome. It's relief, a sense of calm, that washes over them once the declarative statement and decision on boundaries has been made. Someone looking through this lens loves resolutions and tying up loose ends.

One company we engaged with had recently lost several of their key employees. Without those key employees, they had very few people who could deliver the services they were providing. During one of our sessions, we helped them realize they had to decide on a few services to focus on and put the others on hold—at least until they rebuilt their team. Tough decisions, but necessary to manage results and resources.

The Strategist Lens is unique by forcing decisions to be made about internal or external strategies. They allow people to operate effectively in other lenses by establishing clear boundaries. By answering the questions and creating the parameters, they free everyone else to think through other lenses and complete the process.

The danger of not having this lens on your team, or choosing not to exercise this lens, is that you will waste resources. Within your team, there will be confusion because no focus has been established and no boundaries have been laid out. In the culture of your company or organization, it's hard to rally your team because the strategy and direction is fuzzy. It's hard for people to get behind something they don't see clearly.

"What is Our Strategy?"

This lens is particularly helpful when the team is lingering over a decision and it seems like everything is an option. They are also helpful when you ask a question and the answer is always, "It depends ..."

If you ask an employee, "What is our strategy on ____?" and they don't know, you effectively don't have one because the people who need to know and act are confused. This helps you know where you need to use the Strategist Lens.

When you look through the Strategist Lens, you are considering the tough questions. You first have to know where you want to go or the goal you want to achieve. Make a decision on the outcome. That could be anything from how to truly set your company apart from the competition to attracting and retaining the best employees. That's the first step in setting boundaries.

Then, keep asking questions to establish the rest of the sandbox. What will be included and what won't? Determine the ways to win or achieve the desired results, and establish what capabilities and resources are needed.

If you look at any area of your organization or company and you cannot point out the boundaries, you will struggle to answer the fundamental questions of who to hire or fire, what areas of the company will expand or be eliminated, what types of products and services will you offer, will you or won't you outsource, and if you desire organic growth or acquisition.

Answering these types of questions sets up the boundaries of what you will say yes or no to. If you are unable to summarize in one sentence what your strategy is in a given area, you need to get out your Strategist Lens.

Develop Your Strategist Lens

Stop and reflect on the following questions. We encourage you to take time to build a plan to develop your Strategist Lens before reading the next chapter.

1. Ask people on your team, "What is our strategy on ___?" Compare their answers both to one another's and to the actual strategy. Where do you have clarity? Where do you have disparity?
2. Which team members have a natural strength for looking through the Strategist Lens? What questions do they tend to ask that help to define a clear strategy?
3. How can you use the Strategist Lens to bring your teams (and organization) into alignment around a singular strategy?

The Architect

Our companies are designed to get exactly the results we're getting today—whether intentionally or unintentionally. The Architect Lens creates the infrastructure needed to fulfill the strategy. The infrastructure includes the goals, plans, processes, policies, procedures, and systems.

The Architect Lens designs the plans so we can move forward. A healthy, efficient infrastructure allows us to deliver on our strategy. This lens builds out *how* we're going to deliver the *what*.

An Architect thinks of process and efficiencies in terms of a timeline. They align every system with a goal or a strategy. I liken it to highways—every process is designed and leads toward a specific destination or end goal.

This lens is focused on systems-thinking and cause-and-effect. If we want to do this, what do we need to make this happen? The Architect Lens has one question in mind as they process a challenge, face growth, or plan a new product: *How are we going to do that?*

    This lens delivers on strategy within the parameters the strategy has laid out. Looking through this lens helps create the clarity of *how* we're going to deliver the *what*.

    Their primary blind spot is designing something that doesn't fully consider how it will affect other parts of the organization. In a sense, they silo themselves and design without incorporating other areas. An Architect can also get hooked too much on procedure, which can suffocate all other possibilities. The Architect Lens must design processes to get everybody on the same page to be the most effective.

The Architect Lens: From A to Z

The greatest identifying factor of this lens is the linear thought process. This lens draws out sequentially, how we will get from point A to B to C. Architects design. Period.

    If they are good, they will look at the desired end result and then work backward to ensure everything is in place to achieve what we wanted to achieve. They are masters at reverse-engineering from the end and creating an outcome-driven design.

    When you think of a traditional architect designing a building, they first sit down with the customer and get some information. They are prepared to design a building based on the final outcome and the emotions the client wants people to experience while in the building. Is there open space or collaboration space? Lots of natural light or little? Keep the end in mind and work backward. This lens makes sure there's a tactical plan created. They are not the rule enforcer, but they are designing for an outcome.

There's nothing worse for an Architect than when they design and it doesn't lead to results. It's failure. And if it's because people weren't following the rules—designed specifically to get to the outcome—it's a real frustration. They are the rule makers of the infrastructure system. They design something, and they have an expectation it will lead to the expected outcome.

For the Architect Lens, there can be frustration when the Visionary Lens is too big or too loose. This is because it seems like the rules don't matter. Additionally, if a person with a lot of authority or prominence breaks the rules, everyone else does too.

The Architect is simply designing for an outcome. They are not the police. For example, if we want to retain the best employees, but we have not designed a system for recruiting, onboarding, training, and on-going individual feedback, we're probably going to fail on a portion of our HR strategy.

Someone operating in an Architect Lens will thrive on systems, and when there is no system, it feels unmanageable. Chaos.

On the other hand, someone looking through this lens thrives on an understood, step-by-step process in place. When there has been clarity on the expected outcomes and the results that were supposed to happen do happen, it's a fulfilling victory. Someone working in this lens will love designing and exercising their creativity.

The Answer to "How?!"

A lot of times I see an organization toiling over the unknowns. When we bring in the Architect Lens someone will finally ask "HOW are we going to do that?"

This lens creates the processes and infrastructures to achieve the company's key performance indicators (KPIs). They have to be distinct and simple—lean—so people can use them. If they are too big, laborious, and overwhelming, you can't put them to use.

What this lens brings to the table is an outcome that is observable and measurable—clarity. There's going to be a data point, a number, or a drawing that shows exactly what you're going to do. Some of the other lenses are a mindset and an action. The lens of the Architect is clarity of *how*. It's what we believe to be the path.

Lacking the Architect Lens puts you in danger of ambiguity for the path ahead. There simply won't be a clear set of actions or processes to deliver. There will be a waste of time, money, and other resources, along with confusion.

Oftentimes, that creates frustration among people and departments, customers and team members. There may be anger, for example, when the budget is on the table.

Budgets and Org Charts

The budget is at the heart of how resources are expended. Systems and processes dictate how the budget is used, and when those aren't in place, there's fighting or a bottleneck on how the process will play out. Somebody has to make the decision.

Organizational charts and job descriptions are often used for identifying communication or authority lines, and without them you don't know who's supposed to make the decisions. These documents, or whatever your organization's version of them is, shows who does what, when. This creates even more actionable clarity.

You are not required to write everything down. I would argue though, that it is better if most things are documented in some way so it's clear there's an architectural process in place. Documented processes increase efficiency and consistency. It helps when setting expectations and training employees.

Manufacturing environments are where we see the most frequent use of the Architect Lens documented. They design a process to produce a quality product while driving out waste and inefficiency. Less often, there are processes designed and documented related to people, like establishing a culture that attracts and retains good employees, account services, bringing on new clients, or achieving goals.

The goal here is to design and document processes that work together and produce the result you intentionally choose. Choose the culture you want and put a process in place to create it. Identify the experience you want your customer to have when they interact with the company and design the process to deliver it.

Consistency in Outcomes

The Architect Lens is vital when you want consistent outcomes. They define and deliver the outcome and help communicate the results. When a decision has been made, a plan needs to be in place to execute it, and that is why you need this lens.

Henry Ford designed manufacturing techniques that would reduce the cost of an automobile to support his goal of wanting a car that everyone could afford. Knowing his strategy, he designed (and refined) a process that created a consistent product, eliminated waste, and mass produced vehicles that more Americans could afford. He started with his end goal in mind and designed the process to deliver.

This lens is also needed if we believe there could be better outcomes than what we're getting. Thinking through this lens helps us refine our systems and processes. Documenting workflow is the foundation of evolving a process or organization. Companies often look at how to create more efficiency and consistency through documented processes, then leverage those aspects to scale the outcomes or business.

One small private company owner came to us with thirty-five employees reporting directly to her. She told us that all she did all day long was answer questions and solve problems. She could see that people were frustrated, and she didn't know how to help them. All we did was help them create simple job descriptions, design an uncomplicated organization chart, and wrote and implemented a few policies. Those few things, along with a couple of goals that everyone worked toward, significantly reduced everyone's frustrations. Documenting the process got the ball rolling, and now they are masters at designing and documenting systems to get the results.

When, as a company, you know who you are and you know where you're going, this lens helps you nail down the *how* of getting there. Are we going to use technology? How will people be compensated? How will people learn the new system? What will the processes be? This lens will help dig into some of those questions.

Building the Architect Lens

If your Architect Lens is weak or absent, consider an outcome or result you don't like. Draw it out. Write it out. Make it visual. What are the formal and informal processes that are making that happen? Be sure to document what is actually happening as well as what you believe should be happening. Your broken results are a result of your broken processes. Once you've identified them, design one to achieve the results you want.

Look at your goal plan (executive or team) and find the tactical plan to achieve it. If it doesn't exist, then write one. It's just like if you want to make strawberry cheesecake. There's a recipe (think: process) for that. Similarly, if you want to increase sales by twenty percent, there's a process for that.

This is going to seem silly. But write down the exact process you use to make a peanut butter and jelly sandwich. Now, have someone else follow it exactly. What outcome do you want? What outcome do you get? Documenting processes so everyone understands and gets the outcome you want can be challenging.

If there's no recipe, there's no architecture. Everybody is free to get to the outcome however they want. If this lens needs to be developed, test your existing processes or systems. Pick an outcome in your company that is not being achieved. Work it backwards to create the design to achieve the result.

Develop Your Architect Lens

Stop and reflect on the following questions. We encourage you to take time to build a plan to develop your Architect Lens before reading the next chapter.

1. Identify those on your team who naturally see through an Architect Lens. Write down their names. What do they do that indicates they are looking through that lens?
2. What company or team results are not being met? Document the current process. Now, redesign the process to get the results you want.
3. Is your team fully empowered to drive your structures, processes, or systems? How can you empower them further?

6

The Taskmaster

When a fire truck rolls up to a burning house carrying a crew of trained, dedicated firefighters, every second counts. But instead of racing right into the fire, they pause and wait for the instructions from the fire chief.

The chief, who has incredible situational awareness and can assess the best strategy quickly, then gives commands to the firefighters so they can get to work saving lives and structures. He is studied, careful, meticulous, laser-focused on success, and clearly in authority.

What would happen if firefighters immediately jumped out of the truck and everyone ran wherever they thought would be best? It would be chaos.

The Taskmaster is our fire chief. They want us to GET. IT. DONE. And they want it done right.

This lens ensures timelines and expectations are met. A Taskmaster Lens provides accountability to deadlines and commitments. Are we doing what we say we're going to do relating to our goals, strategy, and promises? Are we following procedures and processes?

Peering through the Taskmaster Lens helps identify barriers that prevent goals from being accomplished or deadlines from being met. Working in tandem, an Architect will define processes, and a Taskmaster will ensure they're being followed.

Getting the *Right Things* Done

A Taskmaster Lens is about results and accountability. They want to productively deliver on what was promised. They want to stay on track, or get back on track if for some reason our plan has been derailed. The final outcome is that we fulfill a promise or meet the goal.

This lens has its weaknesses. They can be so focused they can become too rigid and lack empathy. Because they have their sights set on the outcome, they sometimes struggle to take the time to help people overcome barriers. They may not take the time to do pre-checks or establish milestones before the work is due.

Sometimes the intense focus of a Taskmaster means they have been getting things done—but the wrong things. They haven't looked up to make sure the system is correct and appropriate and therefore generating the correct results.

People who look through the lens of a Taskmaster can become frustrated when things are not progressing as expected or deadlines are being missed. Because of this frustration, it is not uncommon to see people peering through this lens start taking on the work themselves—though others have been assigned—just so the deadline or goal won't be missed.

Delegating and sharing responsibilities is a skill this lens needs to develop. Delegating doesn't mean last minute dumping of a task to someone else. It means providing the tools, information, outcomes, expectations, and resources, and giving them the necessary level of support along the way.

A Taskmaster is going to love a good ol' fashioned checklist. There's nothing sweeter to someone looking through this lens than the solid, fat checkmark signifying the completion of one of your to-do list items.

A Taskmaster Lens has a very linear approach to work. They thrive on target dates and deadlines. They want you to get things done and get them done on time. They know who's responsible and who is accountable. They track what is done and not done. They know if someone is off track, and they carry the authority to correct it.

Because the Taskmaster is keenly aware of what every person is working on, those who use this lens will want to make sure everyone is equipped with the correct resources. They take the time to inspect the benchmarks or key stages of the process, then, if necessary, have discipline to correct the cadence of the work being done.

Staying on Task (and on Time)

Someone operating within the Taskmaster Lens despises the missing of deadlines. They don't appreciate someone saying they are on track when they actually are off track. Someone not giving accurate information about their progress is not only being untruthful, but endangering the outcome.

They get frustrated with people withholding information or not telling the truth on goal achievement or promise delivery. They hate excuses or rationalizing to avoid responsibility. They like concrete goals and progress, so it doesn't sit well with them when "pretty good" is an answer for how things are going.

Someone looking through the Taskmaster Lens loves the color green in visual management platforms—because green symbolizes movement forward.

This lens is about transparency. They would rather know immediately if a project is not going well or if deadlines are not going to be met, so they can help provide more resources or redirect. They want obstacles or barriers identified right away so they can be overcome.

The Taskmaster helps things get started off right, and if something does get off track, they are there to get it back on track. They love meeting deadlines and getting everything completed on time—one hundred percent. And that means team members did what they said they were going to do, when they were going to do it.

Results or Bust

The Taskmaster Lens provides several key things, including forward motion, progress, and accountability. This lens is focused on meeting deadlines, and if that means providing flexibility within the project so it gets done, they will. They verify information and push every team member to work toward a goal that everyone can trust.

Keep in mind that this particular lens is outcome and results-oriented—results or bust! It's black and white in this lens. Things are done or not done. On track or off track. Lagging or on deadline.

If you lack the lens of a Taskmaster and their deadlines, you are in danger of high performing employees getting frustrated and possibly leaving because they're meeting deadlines when others aren't. People will be blamed and talked about because they're not performing.

The greatest danger is that tasks are not getting done because nobody is checking. In turn, additional costs stack up because of rework or last-minute fire drills to finish projects.

There is a cascading effect of missing dependency-specific deadlines. For example, there may be five or six people who have tasks dependent upon someone else's.

When it's Missing

You will recognize this lens is missing when you are working on projects you have been working on for years. Nothing has changed, and things are not moving forward in a healthy way.

The talent pool is really shallow because your best people are leaving. People aren't being held accountable to win. That affects your company's reputation. It's being questioned because you can't consistently deliver on promises.

You will experience confusion as to what endpoints or target dates exist. Some organizations just work tirelessly, but they're not organized or in congruence with their target dates. Manufacturing is waiting for months because resource use is misaligned. The Architect's structure falls apart.

The Taskmaster Lens is particularly needed when assignments and outcomes are unclear, and there are no target dates. If we leave a meeting and no one knows who's assigned what and when it's due, that's a problem. If we go through strategic/goal planning but there's no budget or alignment on resource allocation, that's a problem. The Taskmaster will immediately recognize that. The Taskmaster Lens and Architect Lens work closely together. The Taskmaster will be the first to identify when no one has looked through the Architect Lens.

The Taskmaster is crucial when there is no cadence for inspecting or quality assurance. We don't get everyone on the right frequency. We send people to training without setting expectations and following up on movement or improvement.

This lens is vital when people come into your office and don't have a clear picture of what's due and when. In a meeting people may say, "Oh, I didn't know I was supposed to have that by now..." Every task, stage, and phase of a project needs to have a person and a deadline assigned.

Moving Forward

If you need to strengthen the Taskmaster Lens, make sure you know who will do what and by when every time you leave a meeting. And just as importantly, know who will be checking in along the way.

If people start complaining about things not moving forward, which is morale-lowering and tends to increase drama and gossip, the project needs an inspection. Are we certain it is clear what is due, who is doing it, and when it should be done by?

Years ago, we worked with a company who was hosting a conference for about one hundred people. A few members of the executive team had grand ideas and very specific plans on the agenda and the experience attendees would have—the decision makers. They were looking through the lens of Visionary and Architect.

Other members of their team were tasked with organizing and making the event happen—the event planners. They looked through the Taskmaster Lens. The event planners were very organized with lists, deadlines, and assignments. Sounds great, except the decision makers wouldn't make decisions! The decision makers did not look through the Taskmaster Lens. The event planners became increasingly frustrated. Then, at the last minute, it was a fire drill. Everything else was disrupted.

Those who are most successful as they look through the lens of Taskmaster are skilled in their ability to delegate and share responsibilities. When people understand the goals and expectations, they may need help on how to get on track and stay there. They may need support and help identifying obstacles and roadblocks. But the Taskmaster is clear on who is responsible and where accountability lies.

And finally, know when you're scheduled for the next check-in. Be sure expectations and check-ins are clear. Follow up on your one-on-ones and observe who is doing what. You need to have check-ins on your calendar. Every assignment needs a follow up.

Develop Your Taskmaster Lens

Stop and reflect on the following questions. We encourage you to take time to build a plan to develop your Taskmaster Lens before reading the next chapter.

1. What projects are consistently off-track as it relates to time, budget, and/or scope?
2. Who on your team is highly skilled at looking through the Taskmaster Lens? What makes them effective?
3. What can you learn from the bright spots where key projects are successfully completed? How can you use the Taskmaster Lens better in the areas where results are lagging?

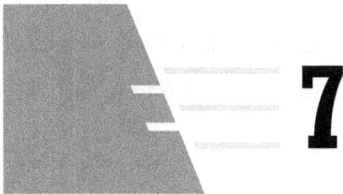

The Truthsayer

The Truthsayer Lens cares as much about the truth as they do the lies. That's because this lens is able to dismiss evidence that doesn't support reality. This lens utilizes accurate information to make the best decisions and asks for the evidence behind a given statement.

If you are operating a business or organization based on integrity, the Truthsayer is vital to the inner workings of everything you do—from your strategy, to staff, to customer service. The Truthsayer searches for the truth and sometimes that means there is conflict. What is brought into the light cannot be hidden any longer, and the Truthsayer wants nothing left in the dark.

The Truthsayer understands the delicate balance between brutal truth that unnecessarily hurts others and the healthy conflict that comes along with what needs to be said. For example: "We don't have someone who can bring in large accounts. What will we do about that?" or "We have eighty percent of the market share? According to whom?"

Strength and Weakness

One of the greatest strengths of the Truthsayer is that they are not on any one person's side. They are objective—their goal is to find the truth so people can make the best decisions.

As with many things, a great strength can be a proportional weakness. This lens is about truth, but it's not perfect. Their primary weakness is not owning it and saying things like, "Well, I'm just being honest." Using statements like this may cause their message to be lost because they sound condescending or are trying to collect the "I gotchas." It's important for those looking through the lens of a Truthsayer to check their intentions. Is the intent to show how smart you are, or do you have a true concern?

With the intent to find truth, there can be times when a Truthsayer doesn't have all of the facts. A blind spot may be that they have information, but the information comes from a bad source or the data is incomplete. Truthsayers must be open to that possibility. A Truthsayer can cross the line at times from necessary and healthy truth to brutal truth that is not delivered with kindness. A Truthsayer can use the truth as a hammer, and every problem and person becomes a nail. Depending on how truth is brought up and discussed, people may avoid bringing up important information, so that the truth can't be discussed or addressed.

The Truth and Nothing But

The Truthsayer challenges statements and generalizations. They will prepare and bring research to a discussion or meeting. They study the industry and search Google, surveys and statistics, interviews, and direct observation. They do their homework. Simply put, they question everything. They challenge our belief that circumstances are the reason we can't succeed. Circumstances are the reality that we *must* succeed.

And because they question everything, there are times when they come across as cynical or as if they don't want to see things move forward. That is rarely the truth. What is really going on is there is a gap in what is being talked about and the evidence or data.

They challenge evidence because people interchange fact and opinion so frequently. They have an innate desire to find reality. If there is a high turnover rate, what specifically is the issue? What is the truth behind what is happening?

This lens identifies assumptions and seeks to validate or invalidate them. It's not about making people look like idiots. They simply want to match people's opinions with data points. They want to find the right goals as well as true data points. It's why they work so hard to gather relevant information—they want to make the best decisions possible. They work in the same vein as a judge arbitrating the truth.

The Truthsayer hates when their data is discredited. They dig down to mine out the facts and evidence that will help the team, and they get frustrated when someone dismisses the information.

What they love is the opposite—when that information is used factually and helps someone on the team make a good decision. They thrive on finding ways to get better data and insight.

Results and Reality

The Truthsayer is driving results by driving reality. There is nothing worse to them than sugar-coated aspirations. For example, if there's a conversation about growing revenue by ten percent, the Truthsayer will say, "Well, we've never even grown by more than one percent, so what makes you think we can do ten times that growth? What are we going to do differently? Is it realistic?"

We have witnessed countless leadership teams who have created strategic plans and goals on opinions and very little data. Sure, there are always going to be assumptions made, but it is our responsibility to do our very best at researching the assumptions to determine if the current data supports our beliefs. Leadership team members must constantly be researching assumptions and opinions. The Truthsayer Lens is all about reality.

Someone operating in this lens is able to balance the harshness of reality without crushing the team. They reveal inconsistencies, remind people of logistics, and stay deeply focused on helping the team make decisions based on hard, accurate data. And they do it all in a way that doesn't break anyone's spirit.

This lens creates healthy conversations. This in turn creates confidence and boldness in the plan. Difficult conversations that are healthy avoid aggressive attacks, high volume, sarcasm, belittling, and lost objectivity. They focus on listening to understand and finding the truth. They are not about winning.

Truthsayers build confidence in conversations. People can trust they are basing decisions on good information, researched and mined out by the person wearing this lens.

The Truthsayer Lens is incredibly important because it brings a standard of integrity to the entire organization—from in-office staff conversations to product research, to the way the company deals with the public.

The Truthsayer Lens is unique in that it brings research, emotional intelligence, and confidence to the team. They challenge perceptions, come to every meeting prepared, and push people to think about how they form opinions, goals, and beliefs. They don't start off with "I think" or "I feel like..." They'll say, "The data shows..."

Without the Truthsayer, you are hearing more opinions than statistics. In situations where you may be discussing employee capabilities, there are people who are not given a fair chance because opinions of them are based on gossip, hearsay, and faulty information rather than direct observation or data. The culture has biases because the Truthsayer Lens has not been used to dig for the truth.

Potential is lost because you don't know what your true capabilities are without accurate data. For example, there was a retail client who didn't believe they could double revenues and margin for the first two periods after Christmas (which are traditionally the lowest). They said they couldn't.

I asked, "Why not? What would you do if you could?" They brainstormed 30 ideas. Some outrageous, others more traditional. They implemented three ideas based on the brainstorming session, and although they didn't quite double their revenue, they improved it significantly, and they did double their margin! They unleashed their minds and unharnessed capabilities that existed.

What Happens Without the Truth?

Without a Truthsayer, there will be lots of blaming. People will either overpromise because of their perception or shoot lower than they could accomplish.

The elephant in the room is never addressed because no one is stepping forward to speak the truth and usher in honest, difficult conversations. There is conflict avoidance and people choose to say nothing rather than start an issue.

Several years ago, we began working with a company who had recently invested in a 1.5 million dollar machine. As they began working on their growth plan, it became apparent that the product this machine made was becoming less and less in demand. No one had done the research before the machine was purchased. They simply did a forecast based on history. Yet as they discussed the future, they continued to include growth goals related to this product. Finally, I asked them why they were continuing to increase the metric related to the sales of this product. The response? "We just spent the money on this machine. We're going to make the product."

That happens. We get emotionally attached to an idea or the money we've spent, or even a perspective, and no one asks the questions in order for us to face reality. So we take action on an untruth, wasting time, money and other resources.

To better operate in the Truthsayer Lens, keep an eye on your reactions during conflict. What dictates whether I win or lose? Am I aiming for winning or for accuracy? What is most important to me?

Do I do things by gut or by research and fact? If research and fact, don't worry about the data part. But if by gut, you must ask yourself the question, "Where is my evidence?" Find more than one point of recent, relevant evidence.

Check yourself. Be helpful with truth and feedback. Be honest, but not brutal. When giving a person feedback, instead of saying "Stop doing X, Y, Z," say, "When you do X, Y, Z... this is how it's coming across. Is this your intention?"

The truth is powerful. But keep it in perspective: it is only helpful if it is embraced by the person who needs to hear it. Communicate truth in a way that can be heard and acted upon, rather than as a battering ram that immediately triggers the defenses of the receiver.

Develop Your Truthsayer Lens

Stop and reflect on the following questions. We encourage you to take time to build a plan to develop your Truthsayer Lens before reading the next chapter.

1. Is your culture results-driven and data-informed? Or more based on feelings, assumptions, and gut instinct?
2. Spend the next two weeks identifying areas where data is the ultimate source of truth that drives decision-making and results, and where it isn't.
3. Craft a plan to use the Truthsayer Lens in areas where reality isn't embraced as the first priority. And ensure that truth is communicated in helpful ways in areas where data drives the bus.

8

The Team Builder

There's a popular game that plays out across America at all sorts of camps and youth retreats. A person stands at the top of a ledge while their team members stand below. The person at the top keeps their back to the people, and at the right count, falls straight back into the arms of the people below. The exercise is terrifying for the person falling, but the point is clear. A group of the right people can work together as a team, and with time, build trust.

This mission is at the heart of the Team Builder Lens. At its core, it is helping to build the understanding that people's intentions are good, even if people's behaviors may not always be perceived that way.

Want to have a strong, effective team? The Team Builder's main mission is breaking down silos between areas. This lens ensures people are aligned with where we're going, what we're doing, and how we're going to get there. This lens works to increase collaboration across departments or offices and focuses on "we are one" instead of protectionism or territorialism.

The strength of this lens is rooted in collaboration and support. Every team within your organization or company should be able to work together seamlessly, and when or if that doesn't happen, the Team Builder Lens reminds us that the inability to collaborate and support hinders our path to success.

This lens is vital to reducing or eliminating workplace drama by helping create empathy for someone else's situation and refocusing the atmosphere to "our project, our team, our deadlines, our customers, our company." In the perspective of this lens, there is no "my" or "me." It's always "we" and "us."

How to See Through the Team Builder Lens

The Team Builder Lens has a keen eye for overlap. Because they have their ear to the ground and a good grasp of who is doing what, this lens helps reduce redundancies.

The people who most naturally operate in this lens are masters at getting people to work together. They don't work in a position of referee, but as a connector, guiding people to work together toward a common goal. They do this by getting people to understand all sides of an issue or rallying energy and support around a project so the appreciation for others goes up. Trust tends to follow appreciation.

The culture of trust the Team Builder Lens seeks and develops is an ongoing process that happens when people and teams are on the same page. It encompasses consistent behavior, compassion, and competency.

The Intangible Value of the Team Builder Lens

Each team member must believe that the people they are surrounded by are competent enough to do the job or can learn. They must have predictable behavior so you know you can count on them. They must have compassion, so you understand where someone else is coming from. Trust does not mean you must always agree, but you should be able to have healthy debate and difficult conversations. The Team Builder Lens helps people discover that people have good intentions—and that although their intentions are good, we're human and sometimes make mistakes.

The Team Builder encourages and promotes strong team behavior, but they have a few of their own blind spots. Because this lens is focused almost entirely on relationships, they can get wrapped up in too many meetings. Sometimes they can be so focused on relationship building, they have an expectation it is a priority for everyone else as well, and other results and priorities can get neglected. Trust can be built upon in a 15-minute meeting; it doesn't always have to be an hour.

Balance can be a struggle for someone looking through this lens. They have to balance between face-to-face connections and large group meetings.

At times, this lens can neglect or forget that team building is across departments, and not only within the team they lead. This is when we might hear the Team Builder Lens refer to "my" team.

A Team Builder must also demonstrate humility. At the helm of helping others communicate better and work more effectively, a Team Builder must also understand they have a role to play in potential dysfunction within a team.

A Team Builder Lens is easy to identify by the way they naturally think about others and the perceptions people have of one another. They think about how decisions affect everyone and as we stated before, their prism is always "we" and not "me."

They are intent on keeping the team cohesive. If we have a goal, what do we all have to do to ensure it happens? They are focused on building the morale of the team members and will be quick to remind teammates that every person is valuable.

A Team Builder celebrates and rewards, encourages, and motivates. They inquire about how people feel and gently push them to do better. They make sure people understand their role in the team and clarify any confusion. When there is drama, they don't add gasoline to the fire. Instead, they ask, "What evidence do you have of that?" Or, "What have you done to make that better?"

They genuinely care about the functionality and morale of the team. They intentionally work to build better teams—to get people talking and expressing their ideas so they can mutually understand one another.

Isolation

What they despise is isolation, finger pointing, drama that polarizes people, and people who don't pull their weight. They don't mind encouraging and building up a team member in a season of struggle, but they will only pull dead weight for so long.

What they do love, however, is people who do what's right no matter what—even if it's uncomfortable. They want to be able to trust people's intentions and be confident they will do the right thing. If someone makes an error, there is grace, because the team dynamics have been built on trust.

Someone looking through the Team Builder Lens will love when everyone knows their part, plays their part, and accomplishes the outcome.

Communication

The true strength of the Team Builder Lens is always having a person on the team whose greatest desire is good communication and teamwork to produce results. Trust may be the foundation of building a team, but communication is the glue that holds the team together. Even if there are hurdles, problems don't have the opportunity to grow when people are talking to each other and truly listening.

Because of good communication, there is simply less drama. Ask any corporate CEO, business leader, or organizational leader—each year there are literally hours upon hours of lost productivity spent in unhealthy communication, actions, or drama. When we work with senior executives and other leaders of leaders, we ask them to tell us how many hours per week they spend on managing the results of unhealthy communications, thoughts, and actions of the people on their teams or between teams. We get answers starting with about an hour per day to at least half of their time. Converted to dollars, that's a lot of money!

Good businesses work toward reducing waste. This is an area where the Team Builder Lens excels. The cost of drama can be reduced when people have authentic and genuine conversation aimed at positively solving issues rather than time spent gossiping, blaming, sabotaging, complaining, making up stories, and generally being disrespectful.

Forget the Drama

Someone peering through the Team Builder Lens will have a sense of discernment. They want to help people express thoughts, even when they are difficult. In doing so, they connect people and break down the silos that isolate team members and departments.

It's a lens of humility. They share responsibility and expect the same of everyone at the table. They point to the expertise demonstrated by people in all departments, and they never feel the need to be the one with all the answers.

This lens is distinct in the way it connects people's heads and hearts. By default, teams are relational organisms, and there's no way to get around the challenges that come with different personalities, backgrounds, expertise, and beliefs. This lens recognizes that and works to make the team a unifying cast of characters working toward a common goal.

If this lens is properly used, individual team members will not have to hog the spotlight. They don't have to be in charge of everything because they recognize they are surrounded by competent people who care about the mission and their customers as much as they do.

As a team, the drama, blaming, protectionism, and territorialism is a thing of the past, and you can create a culture that celebrates and lifts people up. In turn, you have a team that works harder because they are fulfilled in their work.

Are You Missing It?

You will know you have a missing Team Builder Lens, or one that is ineffective, by three major signs: people aren't really listening to each other, there are meetings outside of meetings, and there is low or loss of productivity.

In the first, people will gather information and go back to their specific discipline without taking into consideration the effects it will have on others. You'll hear "my" "mine" "my team" instead of "the accounting department."

The second thing you will witness is meetings outside of the meetings. And by that, I mean there will be informal chat sessions taking place outside of official meetings. There will be politicking. There will be manipulating with a self-serving or self-preservation motive. The motive will be to blame someone else to protect themselves. People think they are trying to solve a problem with another team member, but it's borderline gossip because it's behind the person's back and not with the right heart.

And with people spending time in chat sessions outside of meetings and participating in other unhealthy communication and actions, there is an enormous amount of wasted time. This time is not producing positive results for the organization and may show in areas such as missed deadlines or shrinking margins.

Valuable from the Start

Getting people to collaborate and support each other are great examples of why the Team Builder Lens is so important for every company. They give the space and opportunity for discussion for the people who don't feel they are being included.

The Team Builder Lens is careful to make sure everyone is included during key conversations. For example, they make sure that just because someone is traveling doesn't mean we don't work to include them in that conversation in some way.

This lens strives to make sure every appropriate person is involved and privy to conversations that affect the team, from strategy, to policy, to the company's direction.

They also recognize and affirm the person who is the conformist, who oftentimes can be ostracized. The Team Builder Lens is a reminder to look for ways to include them, challenge them to build relationships with others, and encourage them to do their best.

To develop the Team Builder Lens, we have an exercise for you to try. Ask each person on your team to answer two questions for everyone on the team: What is it the other person does that contributes to the success of this team and business? What does the other person need to focus on to contribute more to this team? Each person should meet with each individual to discuss their answers.

Reflect on your own vocabulary as you walk through your day. Is your language reflective of the "we" mentality you preach? Are you truly focused on the team effort or your own success?

When something doesn't go the way I expect it, do I go into blame and protect mode? Or do I seek understanding?

When the Team Builder Lens is present, you'll see people being lifted up and supported. You'll feel positive energy from people, and you'll hear team members ask, "How can I help?"

Develop Your Team Builder Lens

Stop and reflect on the following questions. We encourage you to take time to build a plan to develop your Team Builder Lens before reading the next chapter.

1. Who in your organization do you see looking through the Team Builder Lens? Write their name. What behaviors do they demonstrate that lead you to that conclusion?
2. Listen to the way you and your leadership talk for the next two weeks. Write down instances in meetings, presentations, or casual conversation where "me" focused language is primarily used.
3. Now, where are the opportunities to look through the Team Builder Lens to create a more "we" focused culture? First in yourself and leadership, next in your team.

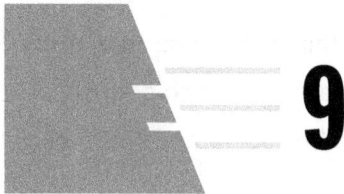

The Coach

It's that voice in your ear—the one that pushes you, encourages you, annoys you, but in truth, simply makes you better. A Coach tells you where you are and points to where you can be. That's why this lens is a requisite for success.

The Coach Lens is about helping someone become a better version of themselves. Someone operating in this lens will reach out to help someone achieve a specific result and work to build their confidence.

Their strengths are varied. They stand in the gap where someone is currently operating, and they point to the place where that person could be. They point out the opportunities and the potential, and then they help the person get there.

A Coach who uses this lens well draws the answers out of you by letting you figure it out yourself, so you are not only thinking about the right things, but you take ownership of the conclusion. The impact of a Coach doesn't come from what they tell a team member, but rather what they get them thinking about.

A Coach has blind spots including a tendency to talk too much. At Revela, we believe that telling is not teaching. You can say an incredible amount of words without real understanding taking place. Coaching—with or without a lot of words—is simply helping someone get to some specific result or outcome.

Sometimes you need the words. More often, though, simply telling someone something over and over again doesn't work. There are all kinds of ways to teach and/or coach. It could be providing feedback, facilitating discussion, or using encouraging statements to help them think and analyze on their own, or leading by example.

We like to use questions and encouraging statements a lot during our coaching processes. Open-ended questions or encouraging statements are our favorite. Open-ended questions often start with words such as who, what, when, where, why, and how. A few examples of encouraging statements are:

- Help me understand...
- Give me an example of...
- Tell me more about...
- Explain what would happen if...

There are many more, but you get the idea. When people self-reflect and discover solutions, there are added benefits. They are less likely to blame others to protect themselves, and they tend to own the solution and are more motivated to act.

Leading Like a Coach

One of the central tenants of peering through this lens is to avoid becoming so in love with your own voice that you lose sight of the goal. The best Coaches understand their place is to empower, not become an emperor. The mindset of a Coach Lens is rooted in leading, but not from a command-and-control structure.

This lens will want to help others accomplish what they have set out to do in a better way. They are interested in helping others be better understood, accomplish their objectives efficiently, and instill confidence.

Someone operating in a Coach Lens will ask a lot of questions, seek to do things in the most successful way, help someone who is not self-aware become more aware, and work to remove stumbling blocks that prohibit people from moving forward.

A Coach hates when a person asks for help and then does not follow through on the action items. However, the best Coaches know that people won't always follow through. The person may not follow through because they get busy with other things or they aren't sure exactly how to go about the action they got help with. They may not even agree with the suggestions of the Coach.

It's almost as frustrating for them when they see people who need help but won't ask for help. A Coach is willing and able to help and feels powerless when they can't.

They never want to feel like someone is brushing them off with a cavalier attitude—yeah, yeah, I got this. They want to help and know it will only be successful if the person is willing.

What they love, what they thrive on, is helping people become better or helping them accomplish their goal. They love seeing the lightbulb moments when something clicks.

The Coach Lens will help people become better based on the other person's individual goals. The scoreboard is always different. It's about accomplishing the business goals and how a person contributes to them first. Then, it's about that person's specific objectives. The key result is the goal for the individual.

This lens is also about improvement. A Coach will not only push someone to reach their full potential, they are knee-deep in the process of improvement the entire time. They will drive skill and knowledge levels along with experiences.

Developing Emotional Intelligence

A Coach Lens is unique in that it helps people develop and utilize emotional intelligence. Emotional intelligence is basically understanding and being aware of your own emotions, and recognizing the reactions other people have around you so that you can improve relationships.

Your IQ doesn't really change whether you're fifteen or fifty. Your personality doesn't change. For example, you're either introverted or extroverted. However, you can manage or modify your behavior and how it's perceived. Though your intelligence is important, your emotional intelligence allows you to navigate relationships and build trust. If you don't have at least a modicum of emotional intelligence it will be extremely difficult to operate in this lens (M. Issah, 2018).[1]

Not looking through the Coach Lens in a situation or on a team means you are lacking the perspective to meet each person where they are and help them become the better version of themselves. A Coach provides challenge. They are not OK allowing people on a team to remain idle. They are always looking for ways to improve and help people become better. They desire progress, and if someone is lagging, they are there to help move things along.

When You're Missing This Lens

You know this lens is not being utilized when you see conflict avoidance and people not addressing tough issues of

---

[1] Issah, M. (2018). Change Leadership: The Role of Emotional Intelligence. SAGE Open. https://doi.org/10.1177/2158244018800910

performance. People are able to fly under the radar and are not contributing. You will see stagnation—a team that is spinning its wheels. Some team members might be passive-aggressive. There will be serious relationship problems because people aren't being coached so they can improve and move forward. There is not a culture of growth and development. The people who are staying are retired in place. They check boxes and move on, but they are not growing.

See Like a Coach

The strategy to allow yourself to better look through the Coach Lens, or make sure someone on your team is operating in this lens, is to take a closer look at goals and improvement plans.

Do you have one-on-one performance, knowledge, behavioral, or relationship improvement sessions monthly or at least quarterly? The point is to develop intentional one-on-one conversations based on performance goals in improvement of performance related to business goals as well as professional behavioral goals. Do the people you lead have goals related to those things? You should always be coaching toward a goal.

When you have one-on-one conversations or evaluations, what is the ratio between telling someone what to do and asking open-ended questions or encouraging statements? What percentage of your coaching conversations is:

telling, asking questions, using encouraging statements, and listening with the intent to understand (not to respond)?

During the next meeting with peers, look for opportunities to coach a peer. Get comfortable coaching a peer who hasn't asked for it. The approach can be gentle: "I noticed that you're working on X thing, and you said you struggle with it. I'm happy to be a sounding board or help you walk through it." Find someone who is struggling and open the door to offer help. Sometimes the best coaching is as simple as brainstorming, allowing them to think out loud, or listening to the hurdles they are facing.

Develop Your Coach Lens

Stop and reflect on the following questions. We encourage you to take time to build a plan to develop your Coach Lens before reading the next chapter.

1. Who are the natural drivers of growth and development for those around them? These are likely the people who naturally see and function through the Coach Lens.
2. As you have your next group/team meeting, calculate the percent of time you spend telling (talking) rather than encouraging others to talk, explain, or share. Without justifying the result, do you think this ratio is effective?

3. Are you using the Coach Lens yourself and seeing opportunities to develop others? Take the next two weeks to work on a path for development for at least one person you lead.

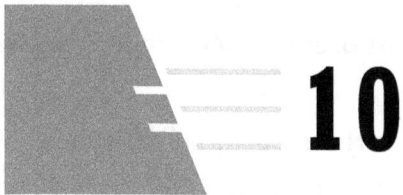

10

The Technician (AKA: Your Default Lens)

When we started this book, I asked you to put your natural inclinations and lens on hold and be open to learning how to view things through every lens.

It's time to bring back that natural lens you put away, which we will call your Technician Lens.

You're always going to be using this lens—it's your default lens. It's more than likely the expertise you mastered long ago. It's what got you hired. It's what you know best and how you operate.

But if your Technician Lens is the only lens you're looking through, you have seriously inhibited your ability to fully assess every situation before making a qualified decision. Not only that, but as we have talked about in this book, each lens offers an incredibly unique view at the people and situations around you. When you can't peer through each lens, you're missing out.

We value the Technician Lens, but it's probably the only lens you need to be encouraged to take OFF sometimes because it's monopolizing your time and energy and keeping you from thriving in other areas.

You can identify your Technician Lens by taking a look at whatever you are a subject matter expert in. That is probably the dominant lens you look through. When you are operating in the Technician Lens, you are making sure people are aware of the relationship that particular expertise has to the business.

The strength of the Technician Lens is that you have someone on every team who is a subject matter expert in something. They will be the go-to person in the business on a problem, project, or strategy.

In the business, they are the expert. There is incredible strength in that—people know you by what you know about this subject.

The weakness of this lens is that the Technician Lens is so honed in on one subject that it neglects the subject matter experts around them and doesn't consider their needs or place in the project.

The Technician Lens will always default to their subject matter, and they might have a difficult time widening the lens to include anything else.

Your Natural Lens

The Technician Lens is tricky. It can be a bit of a love-hate relationship. The Technician Lens is what got you to where you are, probably what got you promoted, and more than likely is where you excel.

You're good at it, but sometimes your Technician Lens ties you up so much you can't grow, move forward, or allow someone else to rise up in your place.

Looking through your Technician Lens has its strengths. You are exceptionally clued-in on how your role and expertise plays into the project at hand and into the bigger picture. When you're looking through this lens, you're willing, enthusiastic, and driven to share your expertise to move the project along.

Because of the expertise involved, the Technicians Lens is often used in firefighting—situations where the problem or issue has been handed from person to person until it hits the hands of the right subject matter expert.

Warning: if you are in leadership in your company or organization, this can be a problem if the problem continually ends up in your hands because you are the only subject matter expert.

In truth, the higher up you get in an organization or business, the less you should be using the Technician Lens. Only twenty to twenty-five percent of your time should be spent in this lens. In fact, the higher up you get, the more your technical view should actually be the other seven lenses. Think about that for a minute.

If you are constantly pulled into projects because you are the only one who has the expertise, you are never allowed to do the higher-level thinking, visioning, or coaching that is needed to grow the company. It's easy to get bitter or complacent when you don't have anyone to replace you in your Technician Lens.

You must create a succession plan to develop others to take on those responsibilities that today only you can do. Without it, you are putting your company at risk should something happen to you. Without it, you are not giving others the chance to become more valuable to the company. It's important to identify up to three people who need the knowledge, experience, and opportunity to become the expert you are now. It's time to put a plan together.

If you continue looking only through the Technician's Lens, the company will not grow at its optimal level. Others will have to pick up your slack.

What's Your Default?

If you constantly default to your Technician Lens, enjoy staying in your comfort zone, and never take the time to develop someone else in your area of expertise, you are handcuffed and will be unable to develop or grow yourself.

As we have encouraged you throughout this book to put on every other lens, we encourage you to be mindful of defaulting to this lens. This lens will be innate to you, so you can't just take it off. But what you can do is recognize that you have it on, and be purposeful to step back and utilize the other lenses as well. You need to breathe, stretch your wings, and get your head up out of the weeds.

I can tell when I walk in the room who has their Technician Lens on because they jump right to problem-solving through their expertise when an idea is presented. When you're casting vision, it's not time to problem-solve. They need to step back from their Technician Lens and put on Architect or Visionary or Strategist lens.

Recognize that you have a Technician Lens but have the discernment to know when it is taking over. If you're a leader, you need to have your eyes open. Enable and equip every one of your team members to look through each of the different lenses. It's why you need to be able to do the same. You can't do that if you're engrossed in an emergency that only you can solve in your default Technician Lens.

There's a pride in knowing that your Technician Lens is where you excel, but the more you understand other parts of the organization or business, the more you are able to contribute at a high-level role.

The great thing about the Technician Lens is that you love the work, truly, to your core. You love the subject you have mastered. You find fulfillment and joy in getting to operate in that lens—at the right times.

If you're immersed in your Technician Lens all the time, you will constantly live in the weeds, putting out fires, answering questions that other people need to learn how to answer. You will be in a place where you can't grow in a way that will make your department and the entire organization healthier.

Reducing Time as the Subject Matter Expert

Stop and reflect on the following questions. We encourage you to take time to build a plan to manage the time you spend looking through your Technician Lens before reading the next chapter.

Action Plan

1. How much time are you looking through your Technician Lens? Track your time.
2. Who in your company would like to become an expert in your area that you could coach?
3. What are some ways to alleviate some of your technical expertise lens-viewing time? Challenge yourself to do this a couple of times per year.

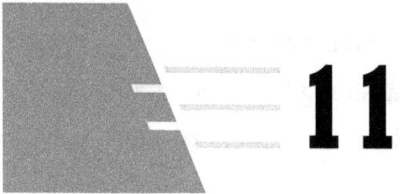

11

The Ultimate Action Plan

At Revela, one of our favorite exercises is asking two people to draw each other. At first, there's always a bit of reluctance, nervous laughter, and then an advanced apology for how the other person is about to look on paper.

Each person sketches the other, and then we ask if the image in their head came out on paper just like they wanted. They laugh and say no. But just like with this book, until you put each of The Eight Lenses into practice, you're not going to have a drawing that looks like the vision of your company at its fullest potential that exists in your head.

The ultimate action plan is simple but requires a long-haul investment. It means slowing down to speed up by using each lens to more clearly:

- Define opportunities and problems;
- Appreciate the natural strengths in your team;
- Encourage and challenge members of your team to look at things differently;
- And lead without blind spots with 20/20 business vision.

Now, even though you've read this book, and hopefully even put some of it into practice, there is probably still some frustration. Frustration because you know there are results being left on the table. You know you have more leadership capacity than you are using today. And you know your people have more potential than you ever thought possible.

However, I promise you this, your frustration will decrease in proportion to the action you take. The silly politicking will evaporate along with putting the lenses into practice. People will thrive in a culture that's excited to work together in mutual appreciation and respect.

The Goal

The best-case scenario is leaders with the ability to look through each lens and with organizational cultures possessing the knowledge and wisdom to pick and choose which lens is needed in each situation. That is a well-rounded, intelligent, talented group of people: those who come to the table with their natural strengths (their Technician Lenses) alongside a willingness to recognize, value, and utilize the other lenses.

Take the time to evaluate what lenses you already have at your leadership table. Where is the team strong? Where is it weak? If you find that you don't have one of the lenses and it will take a while for people to develop that lens, bring that skill to your team. It may be promoting or hiring someone, or maybe it is through a consultant.

At Revela, we work on this daily with our clients. We don't expect your team members to be cookie-cutter representations of each lens. But we do expect them to take the time to view each opportunity through the lenses. That's what helps us be so effective as we work to help people become better leaders and develop their organizations.

This isn't about strengths. We already know your strengths, and we value them. This is about recognizing which lenses you have not mastered or embraced and being more purposeful in using them. We don't need you to be an expert in each lens—we just want you to LOOK.

Finally, allow me to put on my Truthsayer Lens for just a moment. Your work is only beginning! It's time to take action, become more fully rounded, and lead with 20/20 business vision. All you have to do is put in the work.

Don't forget to check out the tools, articles, and tips to help at www.InsightUnseen.com.

Start right now.

About the Author

Andrea Fredrickson, author, coach, and speaker, leads an organization specializing in the development of leaders. She helps people see things differently, self-reflect, and never stop looking for ways to improve themselves on a personal and professional level. She has spent the better part of thirty years researching and developing methods to help people communicate more effectively. When Andrea isn't working with clients, you'll find her spending time with her family and making memories by exploring new cities with friends. She lives in the heart of Omaha, Nebraska.

Andrea Fredrickson
Co-founder and President
Revela
Website: RevelaGroup.com
Office: 712-322-1112
Email: andrea@RevelaGroup.com

About the Company

For over thirty years, Revela has specialized in the development of leaders. Based in Omaha, Nebraska, Revela is one of the region's most experienced thought challengers, helping individuals and companies across the country unleash their potential.

Website: RevelaGroup.com
Office: 712-322-1112
Email: info@RevelaGroup.com
Address: 1508 Leavenworth Street
Omaha, Nebraska 68102

www.ingramcontent.com/pod-product-compliance
Lightning Source LLC
LaVergne TN
LVHW020935090426
835512LV00020B/3363